SHADES of SOUND
Spring

A LISTENING & COLORING BOOK FOR PIANISTS

by
Jennifer Boster, NCTM

SHADES of SOUND
Spring

A Listening & Coloring Book for Pianists

By Jennifer Boster, NCTM

Copyright ©2019 Jennifer Boster
The Playful Piano | theplayfulpiano.com

All rights reserved. No part of this publication may be reproduced or transmitted in any form or by any means without permission.

The Playful Piano
PO Box 12931
Ogden, UT 84412-2931
USA

Introduction

My goal in creating the Shades of Sound listening curriculum is to help piano students gain an interest in and a love and appreciation for great classical music.

Aspiring pianists need to know the literature, hear the greats perform, and be inspired and excited by the great music that is available! Just as writers need to read, read, read, pianists need to listen! Through this fun curriculum, students will learn about the great composers and their works. Listening repertoire selected includes selections from the solo piano literature, as well as piano and orchestra literature, and orchestral works.

Coloring while listening to the music is advantageous because it engages three different types of learning – aural, visual and tactile – and it is something that all ages can enjoy!

My hope is that students can add just 5-10 minutes of listening per day to their normal practicing. Listening to great music will change their understanding of music and will vastly increase their music history knowledge. It will excite and inspire them, encourage further study and listening, give them new pieces to add to their own repertoire wish list, infuse more great music into their lives, homes and families, and will boost their musicianship and expression to the next level.

Spring

This volume of the series focuses on music for springtime. Listen to eighteen musical selections celebrating spring from the Baroque era through the twenty-first century. Included are twelve pieces for solo piano, and six orchestral or chamber works. Enter a musical world of rainstorms, sunrises, bubbling brooks, flowers, fairies and starlit nights. I hope you enjoy this book!

How to Use This Book

Read
First read the background information about the piece. Each piece featured in this book includes the following information: piece title, composer name and dates, and interesting background information on that particular piece. There is also a section called "What to listen for" and a question or two to help encourage active listening and learning. I have also included the approximate time of each piece (according to the recordings I selected for the playlist).

Listen
Search for and pull up **"The Playful Piano - Shades of Sound: Spring"** playlist on YouTube (or scan this handy QR code!). All selections included in this book are in that list in the same order they appear here. I have chosen videos for each selection that are of good quality and will be inspirational and educational.

As you listen, rate each piece by coloring in the stars. Five stars means "I loved this piece so much!" and one star means "I didn't really care for this piece." My hope is that students will find things to learn and appreciate about each selection, whether it becomes a favorite piece or not.

Color
As you listen to each piece, have fun coloring the accompanying coloring page! Jot down any notes or thoughts and answer the questions on the previous page.

Create a Repertoire Wish List
The "Repertoire Wish List" is a place for students to record pieces that they absolutely love and would love to learn someday! I hope that students will get excited about the rich variety of piano repertoire available and be inspired to learn some of the pieces they hear.

Happy Listening!
—Jennifer Boster
ThePlayfulPiano.com

Repertoire Wish List

Pieces I have heard and would LOVE to learn!

Piece Title	Composer

Morning Mood

Piece: **Peer Gynt Suite No. 1, Op. 46: Morning Mood**

Composer: **Edvard Grieg**, 1843-1907, Norway

4 ½ minutes

About the composer: Edvard Grieg is the best-known Norwegian composer, and one of the leading composers of the Romantic era. He was also a concertizing pianist. His style is rooted in the folk music of Norway and is characterized by a great sense of lyricism. His finest contribution to piano repertoire was his sixty-six short lyric pieces for piano.

About the piece: Grieg originally composed his *Peer Gynt Suite* as the music for a stage play. He later re-orchestrated parts of it and reassembled it into two orchestral suites. This work, next to Grieg's Piano Concerto, is his most famous. *Morning Mood* is perhaps the most famous movement of this suite; it depicts a sunrise.

What to listen for: Listen for the flute, the oboe and the horn taking turns on the melody accompanied by the strings. These three instruments were traditionally associated with rural or country scenes. Can you hear the sun rising?

Rate this piece: ★ ★ ★ ★ ★

What I like about this piece:

How I would describe this piece:

The Four Seasons: Spring

Piece: **The Four Seasons, Concerto No. 1 in E Major, Op. 8, RV 269 "Spring"**

Composer: **Antonio Vivaldi**, 1678-1741, Italy

11 minutes

About the composer: Antonio Vivaldi was an Italian violinist and composer of the late baroque period. He was known especially for his instrumental music including over five hundred concertos!

About the piece: Written in 1720, *The Four Seasons* is Vivaldi's most famous work. It is a set of four violin concertos, each based on one of the four seasons of the year. Each concerto is made up of three movements. Each movement has its own mood and tells a story based on the accompanying poems that Vivaldi published with the music.

The poems published with "Spring" are as follows:

Allegro
Spring has arrived with joy
Welcomed by the birds with happy songs,
And the brooks, amidst gentle breezes,
Murmur sweetly as they flow.

The sky is caped in black, and
Thunder and lightning herald a storm
When they fall silent, the birds
Take up again their delightful songs.

Largo e pianissimo sempre
And in the pleasant, blossom-filled meadow,
To the gentle murmur of leaves and plants,
The goatherd sleeps, his faithful dog beside him.

Allegro
To the merry sounds of a rustic bagpipe,
Nymphs and shepherds dance in their beloved spot
When Spring appears in splendour.

Vivaldi – The Four Seasons: Spring

What to listen for: Playful virtuosity is an important characteristic in this work. You will also hear many of the subjects of the poetry represented in the music – bird song, gentle breezes and a thunderstorm in movement one; a calm spring day with a sleeping goatherd and his barking dog (listen for the viola!) in movement two; and a festive spring dance in movement three.

Rate this piece: ★ ☆ ☆ ☆ ☆

What I like about this piece:	How I would describe this piece:

Recomposed: Spring

Piece: **Recomposed: Vivaldi, The Four Seasons: Spring**

Composer: **Max Richter**, born 1966, Germany

10 minutes

About the composer: Max Richter is a German contemporary Classical composer whose works include award-winning film scores, chart-topping Classical albums, solo instrumental works and collaborations with other artists.

About the piece: Richter calls this work "a new trip through the landscape of Vivaldi's The Four Seasons." He set out to find and create a new way to engage with Vivaldi's musical masterpiece, putting his own contemporary spin on it. After it was released, *Recomposed: The Four Seasons* topped the Classical music charts in 22 countries. Richter's *Spring* includes three movements (Spring 1, Spring 2 and Spring 3) as well as one short prologue track (Spring 0).

What to listen for: Richter's rendition of the first movement of *Spring* has the same playful quality as the original, with an added emotional depth. Listen for lots of bird song above a deep, coursing bass line. *Spring 2* pays homage to the original, using the same basic melody and accompaniment to depict the sleeping goatherd on a calm, spring day. Richter however uses a greater range of dynamics and register, creating an even more poignant and mournful sound. *Spring 3* departs more from the original than any of the movements. This movement rushes onward at a gallop, growing in intensity and emotion until leaving the listener at a climax.

Richter – Recomposed: Spring

Rate this piece: ★ ☆ ☆ ☆ ☆

What I like about this piece:

How I would describe this piece:

Improvisation on Spring

Piece: **Improvisation on Vivaldi: Spring – The Four Seasons**

Composer: **Gabriela Montero**, born 1970, Venezuela

4 minutes

About the composer: Gabriela Montero is a Venezuelan concert pianist, composer and improviser. Her first public performance was at the age of five, and her first concerto performance with an orchestra was at age eight. She has performed with many of the world's most-respected orchestras. Montero is celebrated not only for her brilliant and visionary interpretations, but for her ability to improvise and compose pieces in real-time. She has composed other works, including a tone poem for piano and orchestra and a piano concerto.

About the piece: This beautiful improvisation is based on the first movement of Vivaldi's *Spring*.

What to listen for: Can you hear the theme from Vivaldi's *Spring*? What characteristics of the original piece does she use, and how is the mood of her improvisation different?

Rate this piece: ☆ ☆☆☆☆

What I like about this piece:	How I would describe this piece:

Prelude in G Major

Piece: **Prelude in G Major, Op. 28 No. 3**

Composer: **Frederic Chopin**, 1810-1849, Poland

1 minute

About the composer: Frederic Chopin, the Polish pianist and composer, was one of the greatest composers for the piano of all time. A child prodigy, he moved to Paris at the age of twenty-one where he composed, taught piano and sometimes performed. His piano compositions are highly original and full of "faultless grace." His works should be central to the education of any pianist.

About the piece: Chopin composed his famous *24 Preludes* during the winter of 1838 on the island of Majorca, in a cell in an old monastery. He likely was inspired by Bach's *Well-Tempered Clavier* in the writing of his preludes, one of which is written in each of the twenty-four keys, just as Bach's. Chopin wrote, "[I was working] at an old untouchable square writing desk I can scarcely use. On it is a leaden candlestick with a candle. Music of Bach, my own scribblings, old papers (not mine) and silence. One can shout – still silence."

What to listen for: Some nicknames have been given to Chopin's preludes. Pianist Alfred Cortot referred to this one as "The singing of the stream." Listen for the continuous sixteenth notes in the bass that sound like a bubbling brook.

Rate this piece: ★ ☆ ☆ ☆ ☆

What I like about this piece:	How I would describe this piece:

20

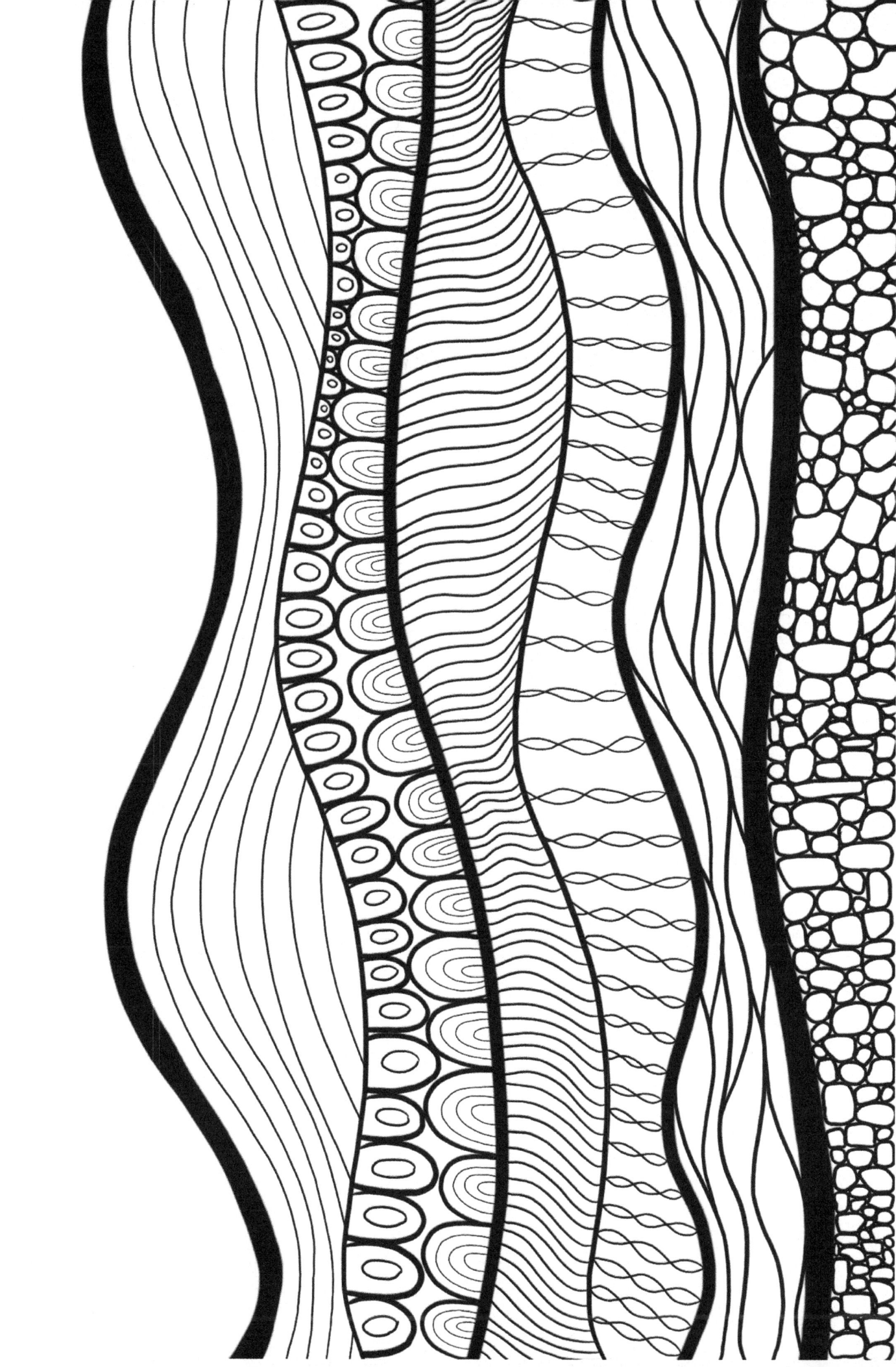

Raindrop Prelude

Piece: **Prelude in D-Flat Major, Op. 28 No. 15, Raindrop**

Composer: **Frederic Chopin**, 1810-1849, Poland

5 minutes

About the composer: Frederic Chopin, the Polish pianist and composer, was one of the greatest composers for the piano of all time. A child prodigy, he moved to Paris at the age of twenty-one where he composed, taught piano and sometimes performed. His piano compositions are highly original and full of "faultless grace." His works should be central to the education of any pianist.

About the piece: This is one of the most famous of Chopin's *24 Preludes*, and the only one that has a nickname that really stuck. The *Raindrop Prelude* is made up of three main sections, the first and last being in D-flat Major and the middle being in C-sharp minor.

What to listen for: This prelude tells the story of a rainstorm. Listen for continuous musical raindrops played on the note A-flat (or G-sharp) lasting throughout the entirety of the piece. The storm at first is light and mellow but turns into a raging thunderstorm during the dramatic middle section. It then calms down toward the end.

Rate this piece: ☆ ☆ ☆ ☆ ☆

What I like about this piece:	How I would describe this piece:

Prelude & Fugue in C# Major

Piece: **The Well-Tempered Clavier, Book I: Prelude & Fugue No. 3 in C-sharp Major, BWV 848**

Composer: **Johann Sebastian Bach**, 1685-1750, Germany

3 ½ minutes

About the composer: Johann Sebastian Bach is one of the greatest and most famous composers of all time, and one of the greatest geniuses in the history of music. He lived in Germany and came from a family of musicians. Some of his most famous works are his *Well-Tempered Clavier* and his *Brandenburg Concertos*.

About the piece: This is the third prelude and fugue in Bach's *Well-Tempered Clavier*, a collection for which he composed a prelude and fugue in each of the twenty-four major and minor keys.

What to listen for: Listen for constant sixteenth notes in the prelude. The fugue's theme is full of optimism and cheer and is made up of sixteenth and eighth notes. Listen for lots of large rising intervals in the melody. You will hear three distinct voices repeating the fugue's theme and weaving them together in brilliant counterpoint.

Rate this piece: ★ ☆ ☆ ☆ ☆

What I like about this piece:	How I would describe this piece:

Keyboard Sonata in C

Piece: **Keyboard Sonata in C Major, K. 159**

Composer: **Domenico Scarlatti**, 1685-1757, Italy

3 minutes

About the composer: Domenico Scarlatti was a Spanish composer born in Italy. He composed over 550 keyboard sonatas for Maria Barbara, the Princess of Portugal, whose court he was a member of for much of his life (he was her music teacher, and then moved with her court when she married the heir to Spain). His keyboard sonatas, composed in binary, or AB form, display a surprising variety and range of styles, emotions and moods. It has been said that this variety and expressive range has not been surpassed by any other composer. His sonatas are often very virtuosic.

About the piece: This lighthearted and lively sonata in C major is a favorite of many pianists. Maurice Hinson says that it "fits the hands well and can be learned quickly."

What to listen for: Listen for two clear sections – the A section which is in major, and the B section which begins in minor but then recaps some of the material from the A section (this is called rounded binary form). Each section is played twice. Listen for lots of little ornaments and trills.

Rate this piece: ★☆☆☆☆

What I like about this piece:	How I would describe this piece:

Spring Sonata

Piece: **Violin Sonata No. 5 in F Major, Op. 24, "Spring," I. Allegro**

Composer **Ludwig van Beethoven**, 1770-1827, Germany

10 minutes

About the composer: Ludwig van Beethoven is one of the most famous composers of all-time. He was born in Germany in the 1700's. As a pianist he was a child prodigy. His works represent the change from the Classical period to the Romantic period. His thirty-two piano sonatas are an important part of the standard piano repertoire, and no serious pianist's repertoire is complete without some of Beethoven's works. He began to go deaf in his late twenties and early thirties and was almost completely deaf the last ten years of his life.

About the piece: Composed in 1800, this sonata was written near the end of what is now known as Beethoven's first period, or the time when his music was based on the traditions of the Classical composers. The nickname "Spring Sonata" was not given by Beethoven himself.

What to listen for: As you listen to this piece, notice how the violin and piano go back and forth, taking turns playing the melody. You will hear lots of expressive lyricism and exuberance in this sunny and cheerful piece!

Rate this piece: ☆☆☆☆☆

What I like about this piece:	How I would describe this piece:

May: Starlit Nights

Piece: **The Seasons, Op. 37b - May: Starlit Nights**
Composer: **Pyotr Ilyich Tchaikovsky**, 1840-1893, Russia
4 ½ minutes

About the composer: Tchaikovsky was a great Russian composer of the Romantic period, famous for ballets such as *The Nutcracker*, *Swan Lake* and *Sleeping Beauty*, and for his first Piano Concerto. His works are some of the most famous works of classical music.

About the piece: Composed in 1875, Tchaikovsky's *The Seasons* is a set of twelve character pieces for solo piano, one piece for each month of the year. The pieces are very descriptive and portray a variety of moods. His piece for the month of May is called *Starlit Nights* or *White Nights*.

What to listen for: The first section is calm and peaceful with warm, beautiful harmonies beneath the simple melody. Listen for more movement and tension in the middle section before the main theme returns at the end.

Rate this piece: ☆☆☆☆☆

What I like about this piece:	How I would describe this piece:

Rustle of Spring

Piece: Frühlingsrauschen, (Rustle of Spring) Op. 32 No. 3
Composer: Christian Sinding, 1856-1941, Norway
3 minutes + 3 minutes further listening (orchestral version)

About the composer: Christian Sinding was a Norwegian composer of Romantic music. He studied music in Germany. Although not as famous as his contemporary Grieg, he enjoyed considerable fame during his lifetime. He wrote a lot of music including an impressive number of works for piano - a piano sonata, a set of variations, two sets of etudes, and three dozen sets of character pieces.

About the piece: Despite Sinding's popularity during his lifetime, most of his works are not well-known today. He does have one piano piece that is well-known in the piano repertoire of today – his "Rustle of Spring." Maurice Hinson says that this piece is probably the most popular piece describing spring.

What to listen for: Listen for a simple melody in the right hand accompanied by a swirl of very fast arpeggiated chords. This shimmering piece is full of energy and warmth – perfect for celebrating the arrival of spring! After you listen to the piano solo, listen to the orchestral version of this piece.

Rate this piece: ☆☆☆☆☆

What I like about this piece:	How I would describe this piece:

To Spring

Piece: Lyric Pieces Book 3, Op. 43 No. 6: To Spring
Composer: Edvard Grieg, 1843-1907, Norway
3 ½ minutes

About the composer: Edvard Grieg is the best-known Norwegian composer, and one of the leading composers of the Romantic era. He was also a concertizing pianist. His style is rooted in the folk music of Norway and is characterized by a great sense of lyricism. His finest contribution to piano repertoire was his sixty-six short lyric pieces for piano.

About the piece: Grieg's *Lyric Pieces* are short pieces for solo piano that each tell a story. They are at the heart of his nationalistic style and are some of his most famous works. They are poetic, nostalgic and charming. This piece from Book 3 of his *Lyric Pieces*, published in 1886, is an ode to springtime.

What to listen for: This piece begins bright and cheerfully, depicting a clear, beautiful spring day and birds singing. The middle section modulates into a minor key and grows in intensity and drama – enter the spring thunderstorm! The opening theme then returns as the clouds part and the storm ends.

Rate this piece: ★ ☆ ☆ ☆ ☆

What I like about this piece:	How I would describe this piece:

Microprimaveras

Piece: Microprimaveras

Composer: Anton Garcia Abril, born 1933, Spain

19 minutes

About the composer: Anton Garcia Abril is a Spanish composer who has composed over one hundred works, including symphonic works, ballets, tv and film soundtracks, opera and chamber works. Anton was first introduced to music by his father. He studied music in Spain and Italy, and then he was a composition professor for thirty years at the Advanced Royal Music Conservatory of Madrid. His musical style is mid-twentieth century with a focus on melody and expression.

About the piece: Abril's *Microprimaveras*, or "Small Springtimes" is a set of five pieces for solo piano. They were written in 2006. The five movements are named with roman numerals from I to V.

What to listen for: Each movement is different. In movement I, listen for loud, exuberant chords and colorful harmonies. II is the slowest movement of the set – it has a more reflective and resonant sound. In movement III you will hear a whirlwind of movement. IV is soft and contemplative. The set concludes with movement V which is very dramatic and colorful. What do each of the movements sound like to you?

Rate this piece: ★ ☆ ☆ ☆ ☆

What I like about this piece:	How I would describe this piece:

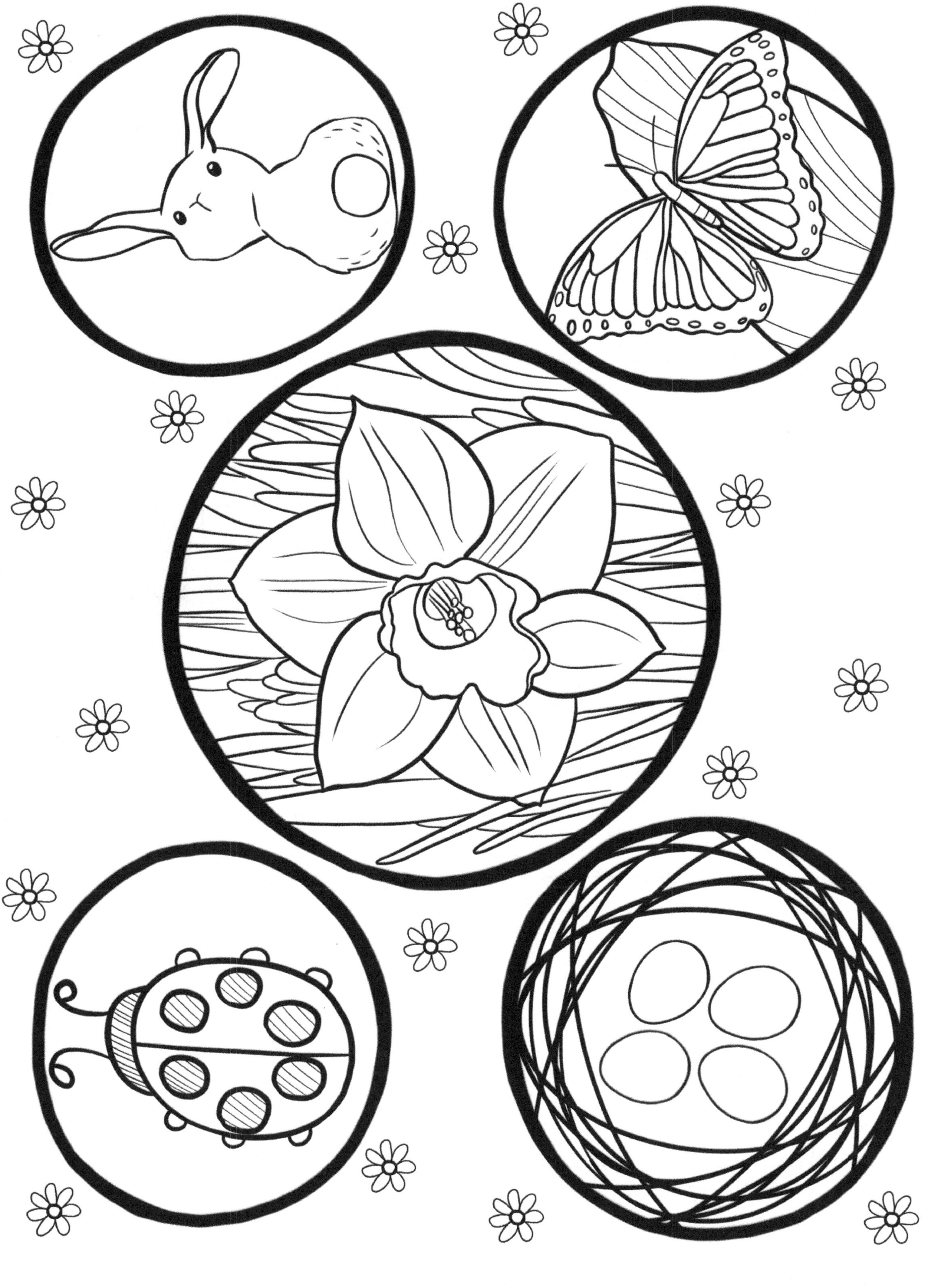

Fire of Spring

Piece: **Four Preludes: Fire of Spring**

Composer: **John Ireland**, 1879-1962, England

3 minutes

About the composer: John Ireland was an English composer, pianist and organist, and a professor at the Royal College of Music. His parents both died when he was a young teenager. His works include choral music, orchestral works including a piano concerto, chamber music, and music for piano and organ. He wrote over forty small character pieces for solo piano. Ireland's music is essentially Romantic in style, yet he was also influenced by the French impressionists and also by Stravinsky. Therefore his musical style was a type of "English impressionism."

About the piece: *Fire of Spring* was one of a set of Four Preludes composed from 1913-1915. Ireland's pieces had very interesting and relevant titles. The other preludes in the set are *The Undertone*, *Obsession*, and The *Holy Boy*.

What to listen for: Listen for some colorful harmonies and a free-flowing sense of rhythm in this lively and energetic character piece. You will hear lots of fast and exciting runs around the melody notes.

Rate this piece: ☆ ☆ ☆ ☆ ☆

What I like about this piece:

How I would describe this piece:

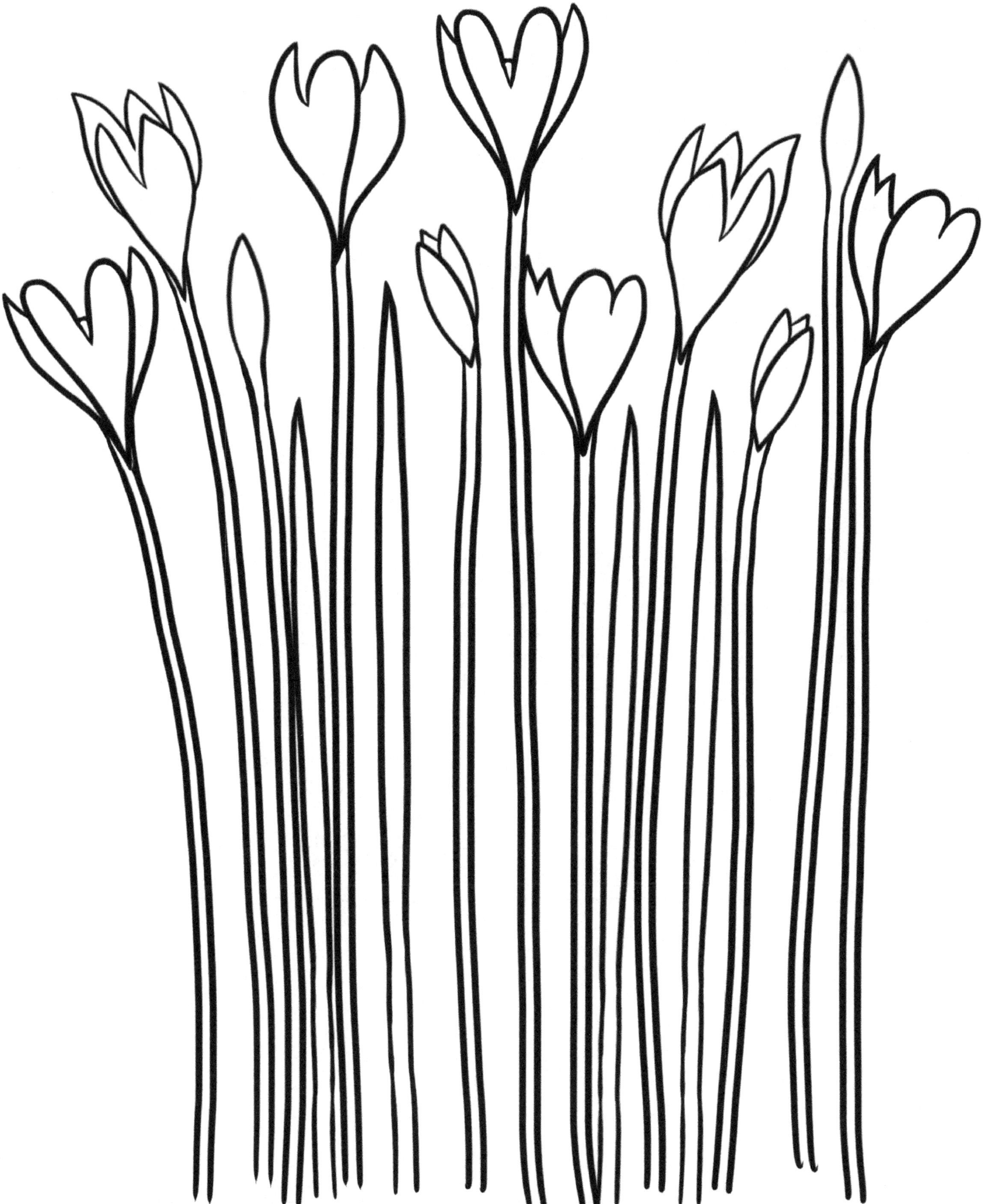

Spring Fairy

Piece: **10 Pieces from Cinderella, Op. 97: No. 1, Spring Fairy**

Composer: **Sergei Prokofiev**, 1891-1953, Russia

1 minute

About the composer: Sergei Prokofiev was an important Russian composer and pianist with a very individual style. His works had percussive elements, lyricism, energetic rhythms and strong dissonant harmonies. He was greatly influenced by Russian folk songs.

About the piece: In the 1940's, Prokofiev composed music for the ballet *Cinderella*. Although this was an orchestral score, he also transcribed much of the music for solo piano and released it before the ballet was first performed. Included in the opus 97 set of ten pieces are short character pieces for the fairies of each season, who help get Cinderella ready for the ball. In this piece, the Spring Fairy is giving Cinderella a beautiful dress made of silver and gold brocade and decorated with precious stones.

What to listen for: This short character piece is full of life and wit and zest – you can hear the Spring Fairy flitting about quickly as she helps Cinderella dress for the ball.

Rate this piece: ★ ☆ ☆ ☆ ☆

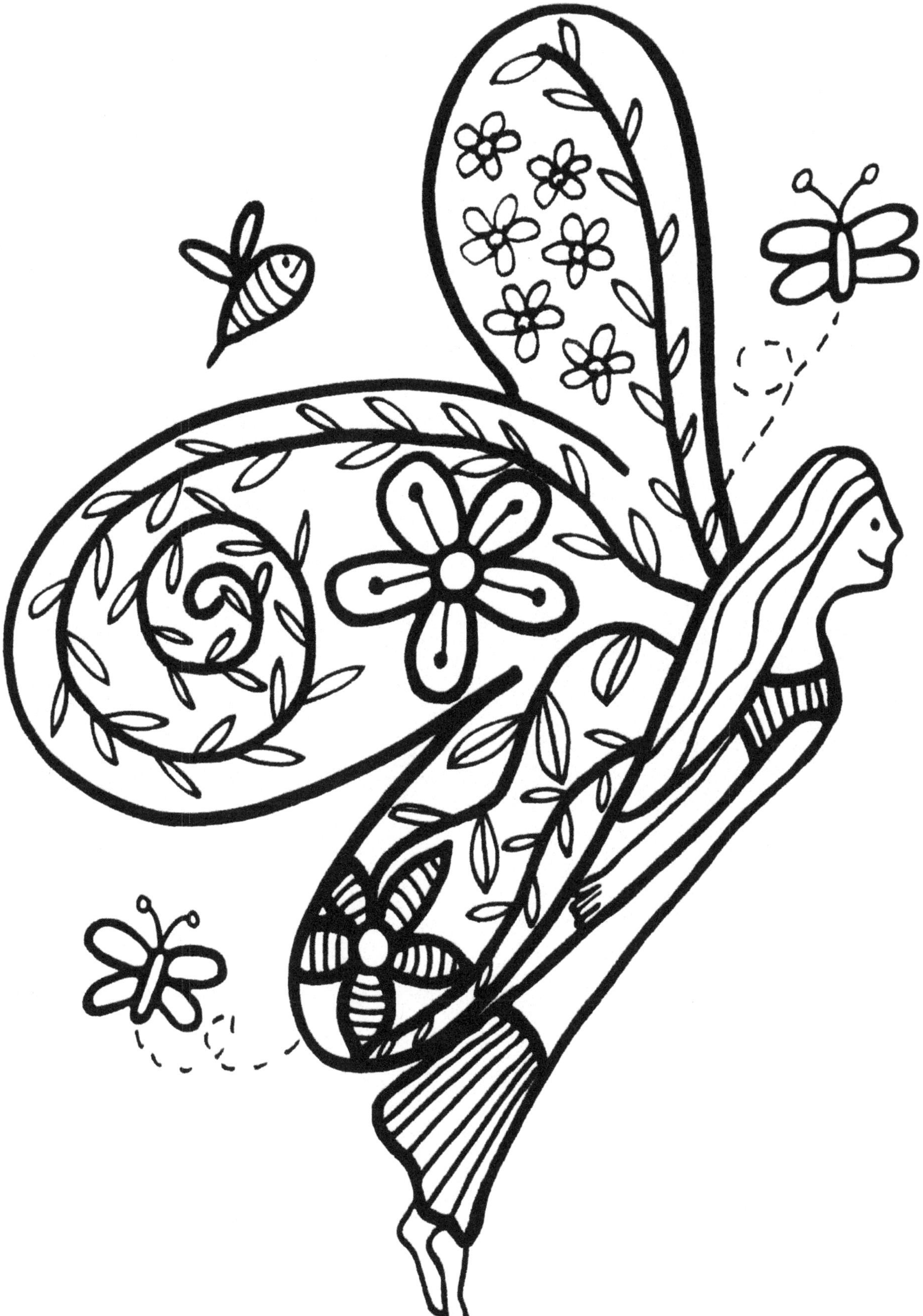

Our Spring Will Come

Piece: **Our Spring Will Come**

Composer: **John Cage**, 1912-1992, United States

4 ½ minutes

About the composer: John Cage was a California-born American composer. He was one of the most influential composers of modern times. A student of Arnold Schoenberg, he pioneered theories on the equality of sounds and the concepts of silence, emptiness and time. He believed that the act of listening was a fundamental part of music performance. He developed the technique of **prepared piano** and also influenced the development of electronic music. He was honored by the Guggenheim Foundation and the National Academy of Arts and Sciences for extending the boundaries of musical art. John Cage was a Zen Buddhist who believed that "good music can act as a guide to good living."

About the piece: During his early career, Cage worked as a composer for dance groups. He wanted to create percussive and **multitimbral** (having many types of sounds at once) accompaniments for the dancers. Since he only had a piano available to work with in the dance studio, he carefully placed items such as strips of rubber, screws, nuts and bolts in the strings of the piano to create different types of sounds when the notes were played. This was how he developed the technique of **prepared piano**. His piece *Our Spring Will Come* was composed to accompany a dance and used this innovative technique.

What to listen for: In this piece you will hear many percussive sounds created by items placed in the strings of the piano. The structure of the piece includes lots of small rhythmic and melodic fragments that are repeated over and over.

Cage – Our Spring Will Come

Rate this piece: ☆ ☆ ☆ ☆ ☆

| What I like about this piece: | How I would describe this piece: |

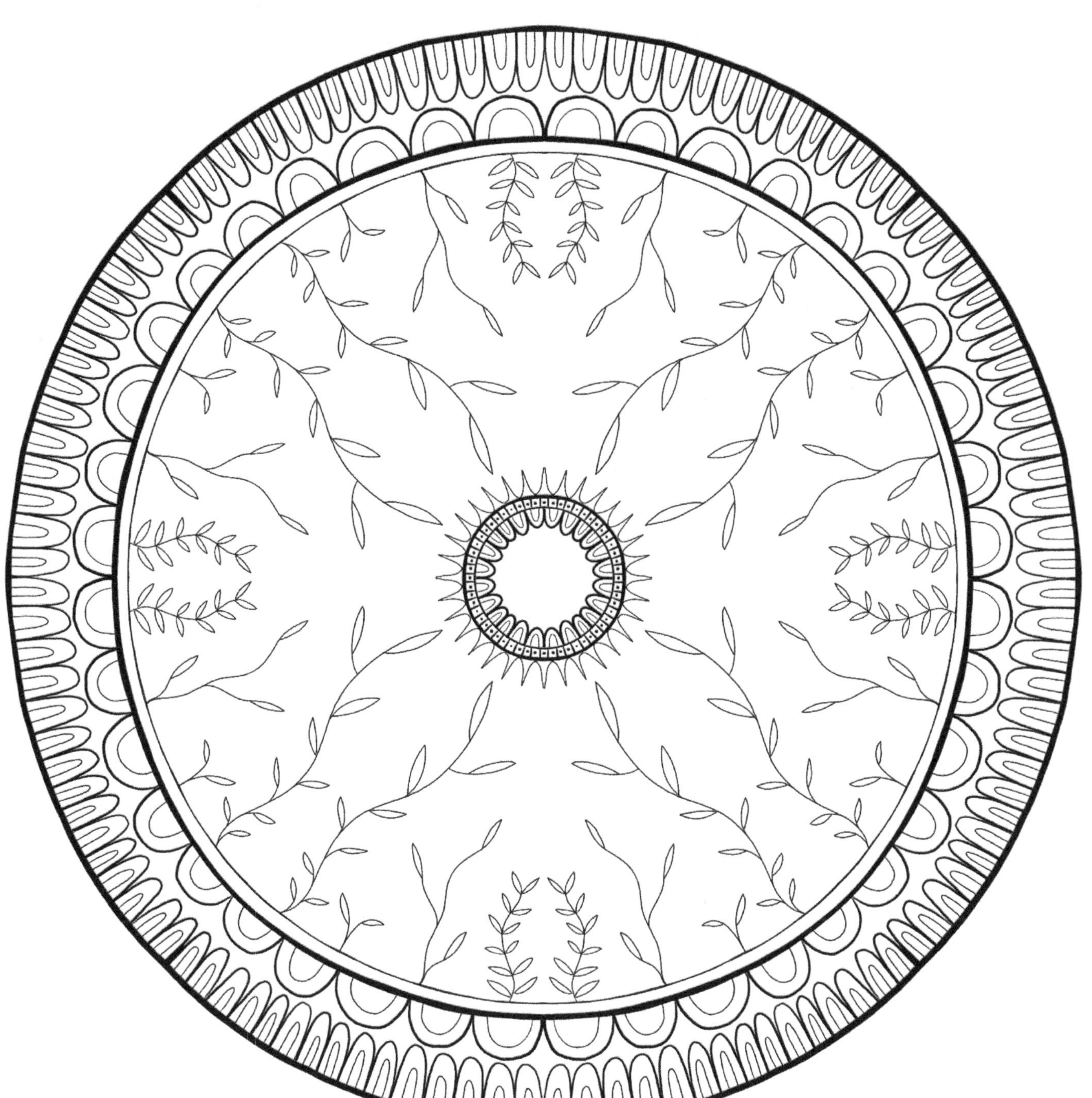

The Lark Ascending

Piece: **The Lark Ascending**

Composer: **Ralph Vaughan Williams,** 1872-1958, England

16 minutes

About the composer: Ralph Vaughan Williams was an English composer, church organist, conductor, music editor and researcher and arranger of folk songs. Because of his work collecting and arranging English folk songs, he became immersed in the song tradition of his country and that style became a part of his own compositions. He composed orchestral, stage, chamber and vocal works.

About the piece: Vaughan Williams composed this gorgeous piece in 1914, but because of the outbreak of World War I it was not premiered until 1920. One of the music critics who heard the premiere stated that the piece "dreamed itself along." Vaughan Williams based the piece off of a poem of the same title by George Meredith. He originally composed the piece for solo violin with piano accompaniment. He re-scored it in 1920 for solo violin and orchestra. Here is an excerpt of Meredith's poem:

He rises and begins to round,
He drops the silver chain of sound…

For singing till his heaven fills,
'Tis love of earth that he instils,
And ever winging up and up,
Our valley is his golden cup
And he the wine which overflows
To lift us with him as he goes….

What to listen for: Listen for a beautiful, soaring melody line in the violin. Much of the melody is based on a **pentatonic scale** (a scale with five notes per octave instead of the traditional seven) and has a sort of impressionistic sound to it.

Vaughan Williams – The Lark Ascending

Rate this piece: ☆ ☆ ☆ ☆ ☆

What I like about this piece:	How I would describe this piece:

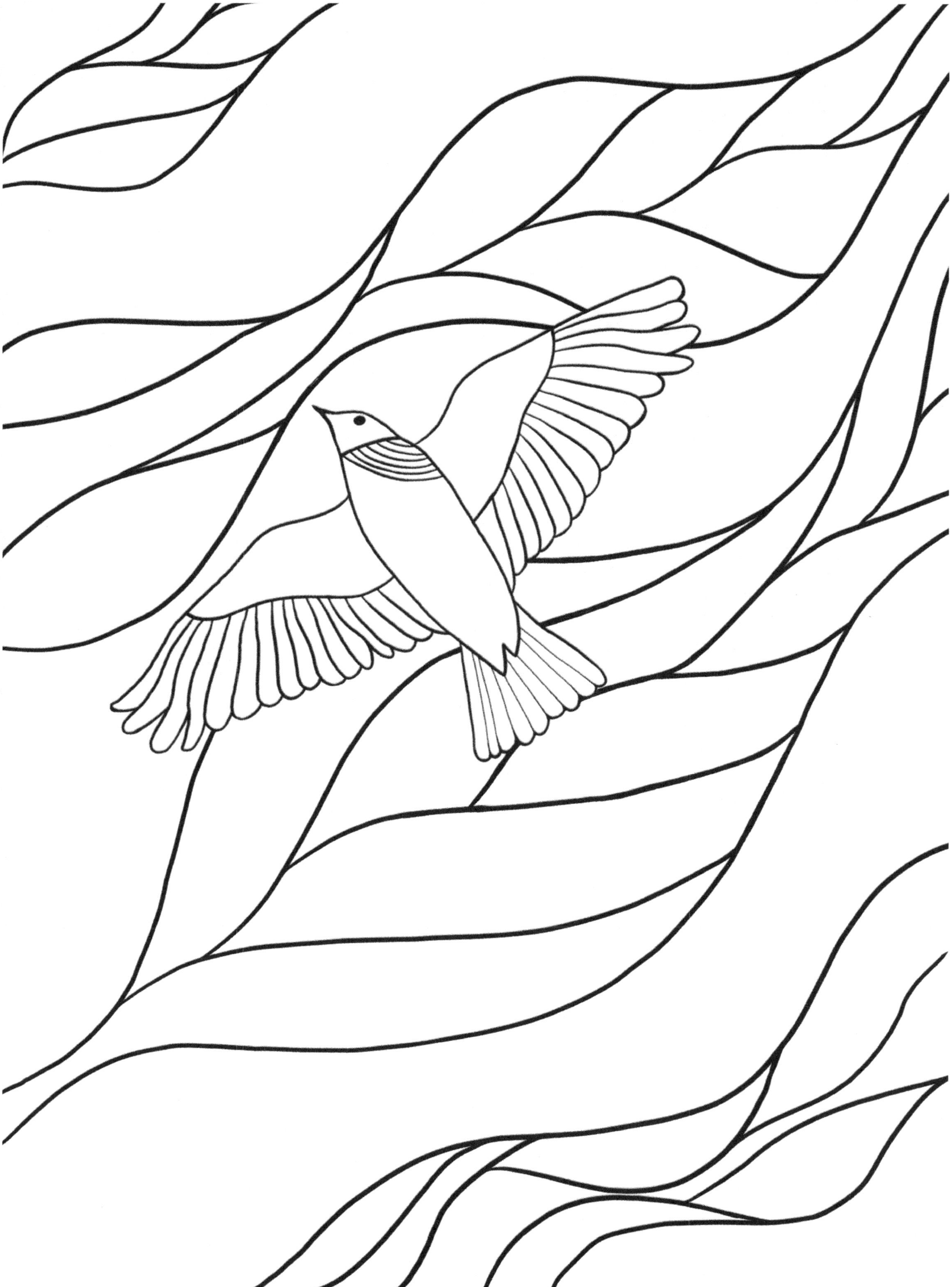

Avril 14th

Piece: **Avril 14th (April 14th)**
Composer: **Richard James**, born 1971, Ireland
Arranger: **Christian Badzura**

2 ½ minutes

About the composer: **Richard James** is an Irish musician who specializes in electronic music. **Christian Badzura** is a pianist and music producer and is Director of New Repertoire at Deutsche Grammophon.

About the piece: Avril 14th was a solo piano track that James included on an album in 2001. The composition has been streamed over 38 million times on Spotify and has been performed and re-recorded by several other artists. Badzura arranged the piece for violin, piano, double bass, harp and string quartet for violinist Daniel Hope's classical album *For Seasons*.

What to listen for: Listen for warm harmonies that evoke the thaw of winter into springtime. You will hear some fun textures created by the combination of instruments and the varied treatment of notes – from smooth and legato to short **pizzicato** (plucked strings), like raindrops falling in an April rainstorm.

Rate this piece: ☆ ☆ ☆ ☆ ☆

What I like about this piece:	How I would describe this piece:

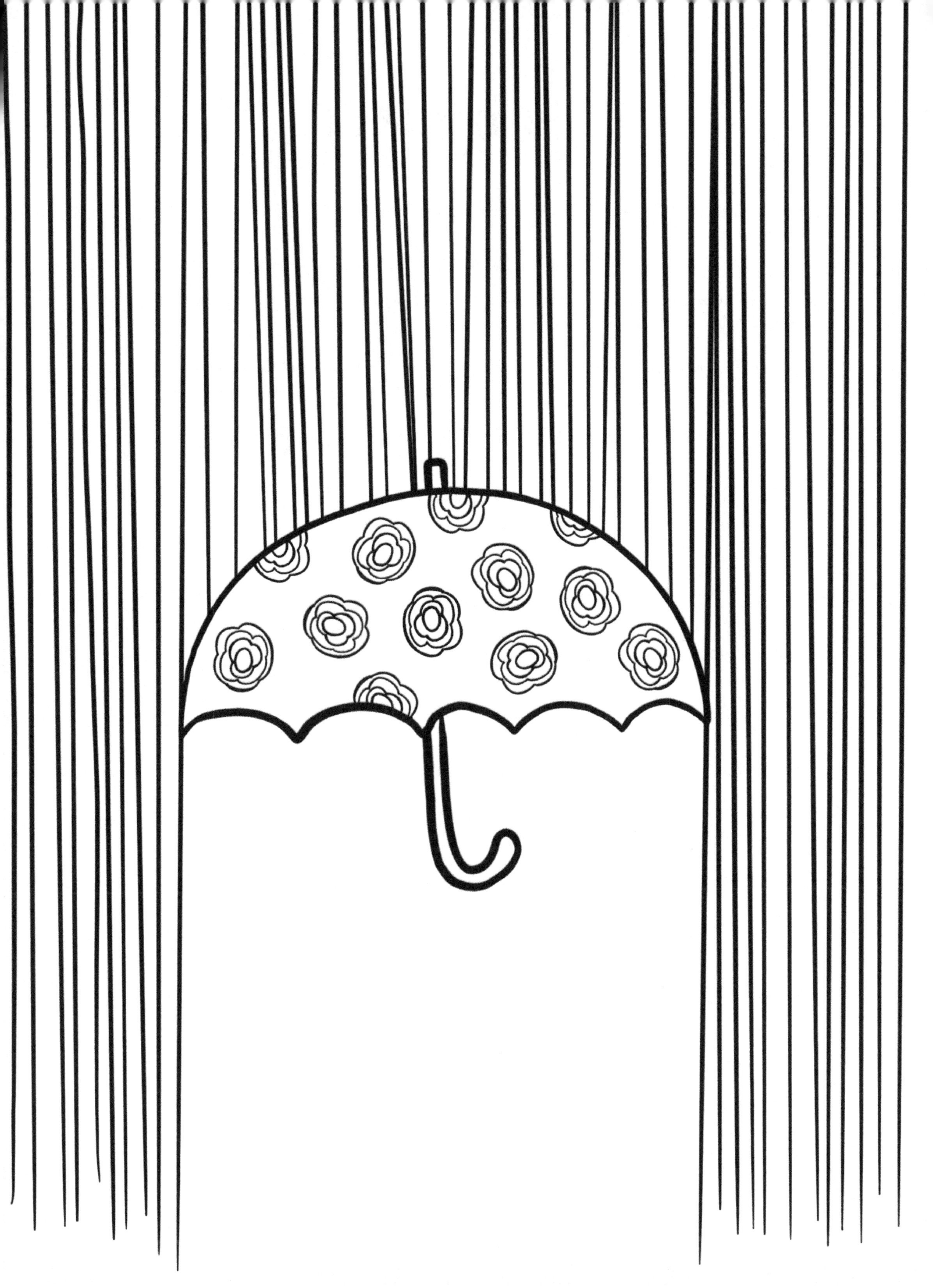

Bibliography

Aspen Music Festival. "Ludwig Van Beethoven: Violin Sonata No. 5 in F Major, op. 24, 'Spring.'" Aspenmusicfestival.com. http://www.aspenmusicfestival.com/program_notes/view/beethoven-violin-sonata-no.-5-in-f-major-op.-24-spring (Accessed April 8, 2019).

Burton-Hill, Clemency. *Year of Wonder: Classical Music to Enjoy Day by Day.* New York, New York: HarperCollins Publishers, 2018.

Classic FM. "How I Wrote… Vivaldi's Four Seasons Recomposed – Max Richter." Classicfm.com. https://www.classicfm.com/composers/richter/news/vivaldi-recomposed-interview/ (Accessed February 6, 2019).

Classic FM. "The Story Behind Edvard Grieg's Peer Gynt." Classicfm.com. https://www.classicfm.com/composers/grieg/guides/story-behind-griegs-peer-gynt/ (Accessed April 4, 2019.)

Gabriela Montero. "Gabriela Montero: Biography." Gabrielamontero.com. https://www.gabrielamontero.com/biography (Accessed February 6, 2019).

Gengaro, Christine Lee. "Program Notes: Four Seasons." Los Angeles Chamber Orchestra. Archived from the original on 15 July 2012.

Gordon, Stewart. *A History of Keyboard Literature: Music for the Piano and its Forerunners.* Belmont, California: Wadsworth Group/Thomson Learning, 1996.

Hinson, Maurice, and Wesley Roberts. *Guide to the Pianist's Repertoire*, Fourth Edition, Kindle Edition. Bloomington: Indiana University Press, 2014.

Huneker, James. *Chopin: The Man and His Music.* Dover Publications, 1966.

Max Richter Music. "Max Richter: Bio." Maxrichtermusic.com. https://www.maxrichtermusic.com/bio/ (Accessed February 6, 2019).

Palmer, Willard A., ed. "Chopin Preludes for the Piano." Alfred Publishing Co., Inc., 1992.

Randel, Don Michael, ed. *The Harvard Concise Dictionary of Music and Musicians.* Cambridge, Massachusetts: The Belknap Press of Harvard University Press, 1999.

Schwarm, Betsy. "The Four Seasons by Vivaldi." Britannica.com. https://www.britannica.com/topic/The-Four-Seasons-by-Vivaldi (Accessed February 6, 2019).

Spain is Culture. "Anton Garcia Abril." Spainisculture.com. http://www.spainisculture.com/en/artistas_creadores/anton_garcia_abril.html (Accessed May 3, 2019).

Did you enjoy this book?
Please help me get the word out by
leaving me an Amazon review!

Check out the other Shades of Sound Listening &
Coloring Books in the series!

Listening &
Coloring
Books

Shades of Sound: Women Composers
Shades of Sound: Winter
Shades of Sound: Notre Dame
Shades of Sound: Halloween
Shades of Sound: Thanksgiving
Shades of Sound: Christmas
Shades of Sound: New Year's Day
Shades of Sound: Valentine's Day
More titles coming soon!

About the Author

Jenny Boster has been playing the piano and drawing ever since she was a little girl. She loves combining her interests to create fun and original resources for piano teachers. She has loved teaching piano lessons for twenty years! Jenny has a Bachelor of Music degree in Piano Performance from Brigham Young University and is a Nationally-Certified Teacher of Music. Jenny is passionate about encouraging students to listen to and gain a love for classical music. Her greatest joys are her husband, Jonathan, and being a mother to her five children.

Made in the USA
Las Vegas, NV
02 May 2022